IF HE'S UP TO SOMETHING, I'LL KICK MYSELF FOR LETTING HIM GO!... ERK!
OO...ER! SORRY, SUPERTED! LOOKS LIKE I'VE KICKED YOU!

BUBBLING BLANCMANGE! NOW SPOTTY'S IN A FLAT SPIN!

ULP!
AND SO IS EVERYONE ELSE WEARING THOSE BOOTS! I'LL BET TEX IS GETTING A KICK OUT OF THIS!
OO...ER!
YEOW!

SURE ENOUGH...
HAW-HAW! THIS 'CHAOS CONTROL' MAKES ALL THEM THAR BOOTS-AND WHOEVER'S WEAR-ING THEM-GO WILD!
YOU REALLY ENJOY BEING A HEEL, DON'T YOU, BOSS?

MEANWHILE...
D...DO SOMETHING SUPERTED! I C...CAN GET THESE BOOTS OFF!
NOR CA ANYONE ELS TIME FOR M OFF! BU BACK

AND...
THANKS FOR YOUR HELP, MR. GUMM!
YOU'RE WELCOME, SUPERTED!
IVOR GUMM GLUE

SUPER-STRONG GLUE–WHAT BETTER WAY TO MAKE SPOTTY AND THE OTHERS...
GLUG!

...STICK AROUND!
NICE WORK, SUPERTED! NOW PULL ME OUT OF THESE BOOTS!

SUPERTED AND SPOTTY FREE EVERYONE ELSE. THEN...
HURRY, SPOTTY! IT'S TEX'S TURN TO COME UNSTUCK!
HE WENT THAT WAY, SUPERTED!

MY BOOTS WERE MADE FOR... M-I-S-C-H-I-E-F!
OH, NO! B...BOSS, IT'S SUPERTED!

TEX FOOLED US! NOW IT'S HIS TURN TO SEE SOMETHING FALL!
THIS SHOULD BE A BARREL OF LAUGHS!

SUPERTED ANNUAL 1992 is published by THE REDAN COMPANY, 29 St John's Lane, London EC1M 4BJ. Printed in Italy.

£4.50

LOOK OUT, BOSS!
EH?
KER-UMP!

W...WHAT HAPPENED?
WE'RE NOT MOVING - WHY?
HEAR THAT, SPOTTY? THEY'RE SO SHAKEN UP, THEY HAVEN'T A GLUE!

CLEAN UP, EVERY DROP OF GLUE, TEX! AT LEAST YOU'RE WEARING NICE, DRY GUMBOOTS! HA-HA!
OUR NEW YEAR'S RESOLUTION IS TO MAKE SURE HE DOESN'T GET TOO BIG FOR HIS BOOTS AGAIN!

The tree moved, a crooked branch reached out and long weird, leafy fingers descended. . .

Mystery In The Park!

"Dad! That tree!" began the little boy, pointing. "It's **moving!**"

"You and your imagination, Jimmy!" grinned his Dad. "Come and play catch – we're waiting for you!"

Jimmy frowned, took a final glance at the tree and then turned to catch the ball that his father threw to him.

"To me next, Jimmy!" called his sister, Sally. "Mum's waiting, too!"

"Just five more minutes – then we'll all have our picnic!" smiled Mum. "Really, Jimmy! Walking trees! Whatever will you dream up next?"

The family left a blanket on the ground, near their car, with a picnic hamper on it. Jimmy soon forgot the tree as he threw the ball. There was no way he could have heard the faintest of rustling sounds from the tree, as a long, crooked branch reached out, its tip like weird, leafy fingers. . .

"Mum, our picnic hamper! It's **vanished**!" called Jimmy's sister, when their game was over.

"That's impossible!" said Mum, hurrying over to their picnic spot.

"Not if someone stole it when we weren't looking!" frowned Dad. "Come on. We'd better tell the police!"

Jimmy glanced at the tree. **Had** it moved farther away again, or was he imagining it? Certainly, its thick, gnarled trunk looked creepy and reminded him of a film he'd seen about a **magic** forest – where trees came to life! But, for now, he kept quiet. He didn't want everyone laughing at him again.

Elsewhere in the city park, a lady relaxed in her deckchair under the shade of a tall bush. She soon fell asleep. So she could not have seen the bush suddenly begin to lean forward towards her handbag which hung from the back of the chair. And, not far away, a fisherman sat beside the park lake. Nearby, was another bush, this one big and round, with trumpet-like flowers.
Suddenly, the fisherman's line went taut and, for a moment, he struggled to land a fish on the end. He was too busy and excited to notice one of the bush's flowers moving on its stretching stem towards his lunch-box. Like a suction-pad, the flower settled. Seconds later, the fisherman had lost the fish again – and, to his surprise, his lunch-box. It had completely disappeared!

"Ha-ha-ha! Tee-hee-hee!" chuckled SuperTed and Spotty meanwhile, as they stood under the water fountain. "This ... ho-ho-ho! ... is the best laugh ... tee-hee! ... I've had in ages!" said SuperTed.

"I thought ... ha-ha! ... you'd enjoy ... ho-ho! ... the giggle-spray springs on Planet Tickle!" replied Spotty.

When they had laughed so much that their sides ached, the two friends stepped clear of the spray and dried themselves.

"Coming here is a real **laugh**!" agreed SuperTed. "But I think it's time we were getting back to the space station!"

Spotty fetched a small bottle from the spotty rocket and filled it with giggle-spray. "I'll take this with me," he said, "in case we want some more fun!"

Then they sped off aboard the spotty rocket and soon reached the space station above Earth. As they arrived, an urgent message was coming through on the video monitor: *"This is the City Chief of Police. Come in, SuperTed. . !"*

The Superbear stayed just long to hear about the strange thefts in city park. Then he and Spotty took off again and flew straight there.

"Things have vanished from all over the park!" SuperTed told Spotty. "There are even stranger reports of a moving tree and bushes!"

"I can't think what's behind it all!" frowned the Police Chief who met them at the park entrance.

"Or **who**!" added SuperTed. "I've a hunch it could be that crooked cowboy Texas Pete and his gang!" The Superbear glanced thoughtfully at a park-keeper spraying roses and remembered Spotty's bottle of giggle-spray. "I mean to find out!"

At that moment, Tex peered through the knot hole in the trunk of his mechanical tree disguise. He could see SuperTed and Spotty talking to the police chief. "Tex calling Bulk and Skeleton!" he whispered into a radio. "It's time we **branched** out and went for easy **pickings** elsewhere!"

"Right, boss!" replied Skeleton, from his tall bush disguise.

"Meddling with SuperTed is **no picnic**!"

"I've . . . munch! . . . just eaten one!" added Bulk, speaking into his radio from the special flower-shrub where he was hiding.

That moment, SuperTed and Spotty flew low over the park, spraying all the trees and bushes in sight.

"I hope this works!" said Spotty.

"Cheer up, Spotty!" grinned SuperTed. "Or I'll spray you! I've just those two shrubs and that tree over there to go now!"

Tex, Bulk and Skeleton froze as they heard SuperTed and Spotty zooming closer. "They're sure to **leaf** us alone in these disguises!" Tex chuckled quietly over the radio-link. But then he began to laugh louder and louder. He could not stop himself! Neither could Bulk nor Skeleton.

"Sssh! Be...ha-ha!...quiet...haw-haw!" Tex yelled to the others, over the radio. Tears of laughter began to run down his face, until he could not see where he was going and he tripped over. Nearby, Bulk was rolling on his back, kicking his feet in the air as he, too, laughed until he burst out of his disguise – which was not too hard for him to do, anyway! Meanwhile, Skeleton giggled and chuckled so his bones rattled, giving him away.

Onlookers stared in amazement at all the stolen valuables that fell out of the disguises, too. The villains were still laughing helplessly while SuperTed and Spotty tied up all three of them in a hosepipe, until the police chief and his men arrived.

"Nice work, SuperTed!" said the police chief.

"That's another case **wound up**!" grinned Spotty.

"Gah! My plan...haw-haw!...ruined...ha-ha!...!" began Tex.

"It was easy, thanks to the giggle-spray we soaked you in!" said SuperTed. "But don't worry, the effect will soon wear off – just like your disguises! But I have to admit, Tex, yours was **tree-mendous**! Ha-ha-ha!"

The End

Island Hop
PIRATE ISLE
MISS A TURN!
An exciting game for two or more players.

Help Super Ted find the loot on Treasure Island before Texas Pete and his gang! All you need to play **Island Hop** is a dice and coloured counters or buttons. Take it in turns to throw the dice and move the number of squares shown. The first player to reach **Treasure Isle** wins the game – but be careful – there are plenty of traps on the way!

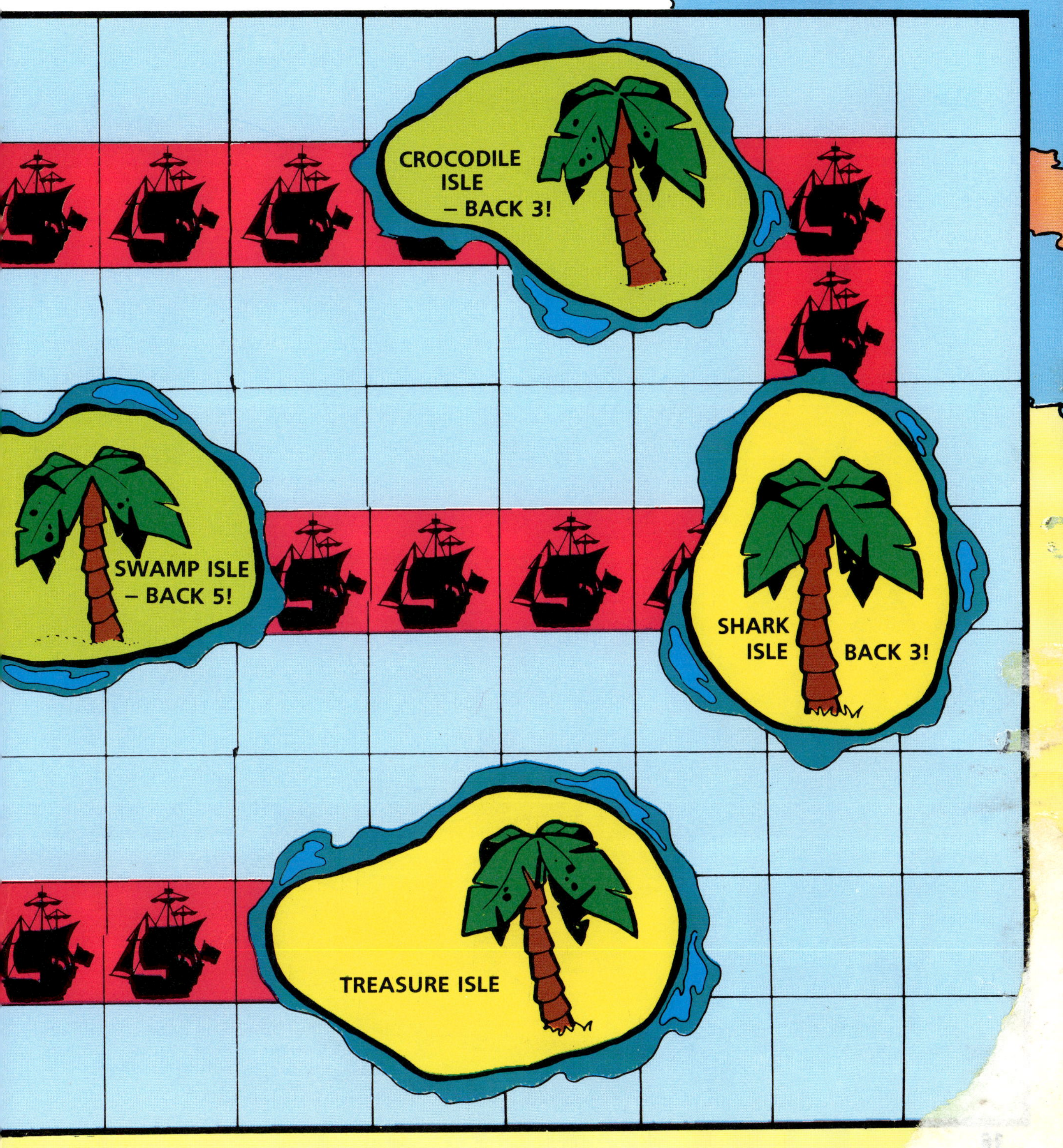

Oh dear! Super Ted has lost his way on the **Planet Maze.** Help him to find his way back to Spotty Man without bumping into the Maze Spooks who live there!

THE PLANET MAZE

Space Witch
One day, when SuperTed and Spotty arrived back at the treehouse. . .
Where have all these frogs come from?
Great Moons of Spot! They're everywhere!

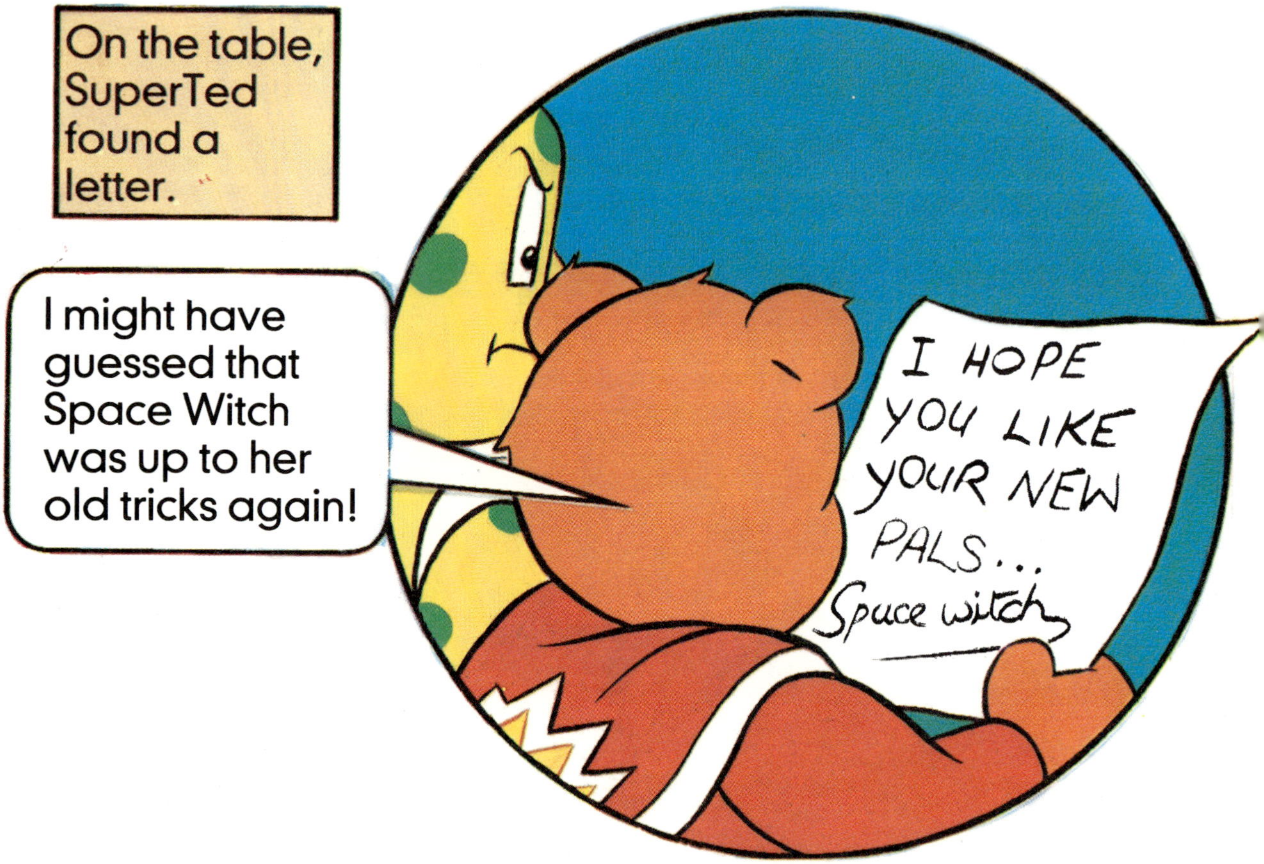

On the table, SuperTed found a letter.

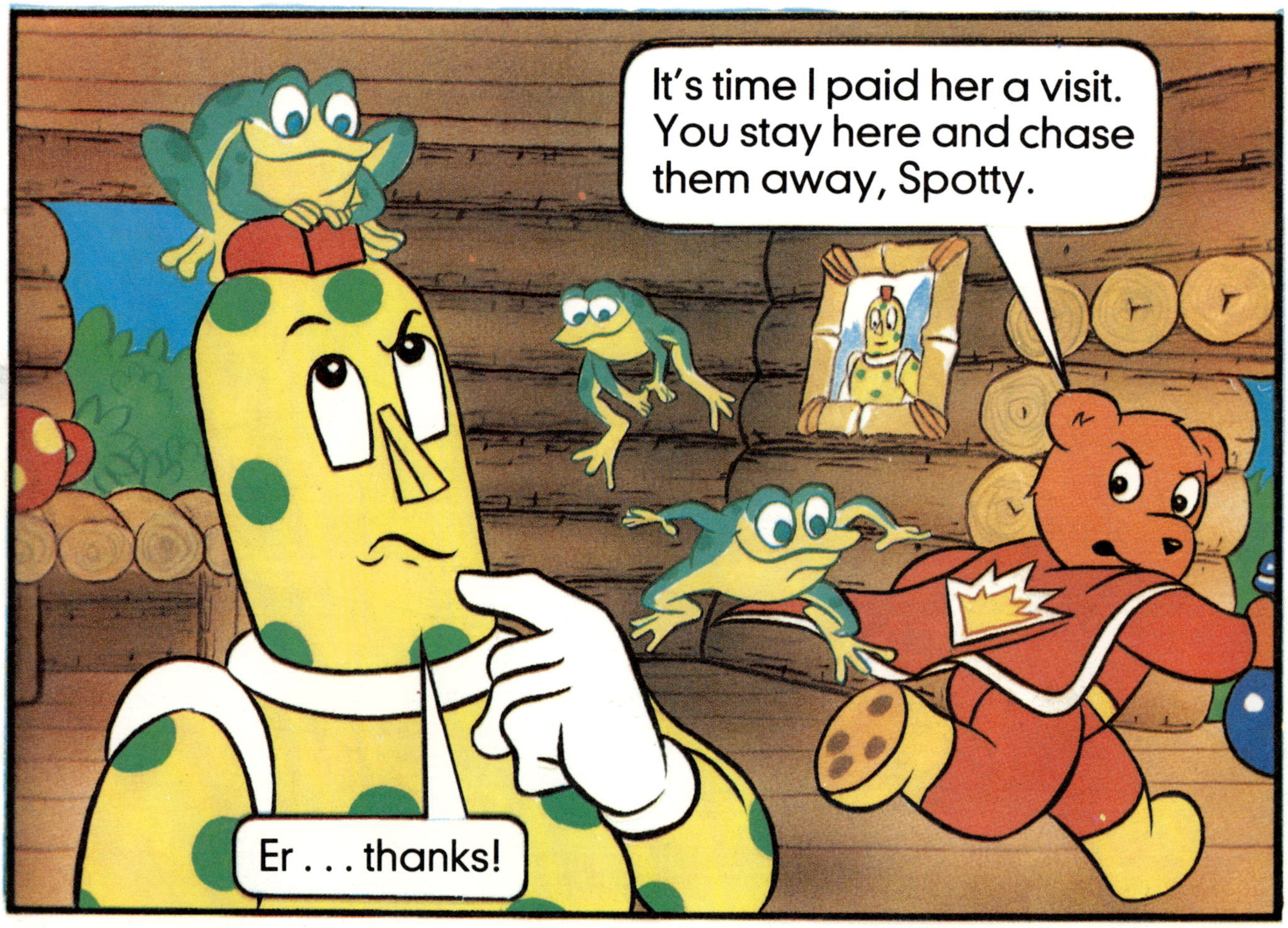

Armed with his cosmic dust, SuperTed began to search for the Space Witch. . .

Now where can she be?

SuperTed tried all the gloomy places he could think of, but there was no sign of her.

Oh, well. I'd better keep looking.

The only place SuperTed had not tried was a creepy castle . . .

Crumbling comets! What sort of bird is that?

He soon had an even bigger surprise . . .

Dinosaurs! But there are no dinosaurs these days!

When SuperTed tried to push one of the monsters away . . .

Inside the castle . . .
Just as I thought. She's using her magic ball again.

Bubbling blancmange!
It isn't real!
It did not take him long to guess what was happening.
There is only one person who would spook up creatures like that. Where's that witch?

Hee-hee!
A few more
and I'll have
an army of
dinosaurs.

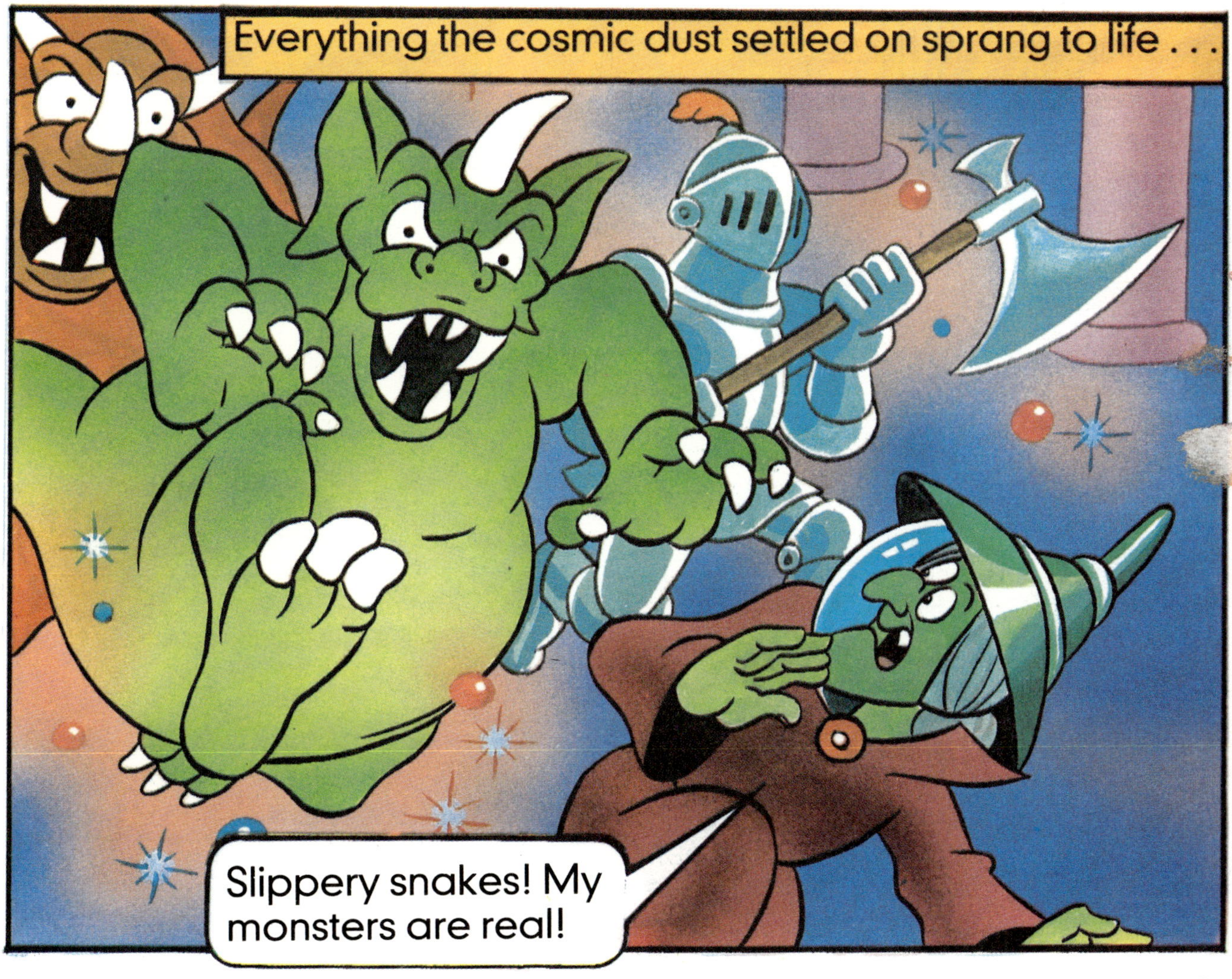

Everything the cosmic dust settled on sprang to life . . .

Slippery snakes! My monsters are real!

Then SuperTed sprinkled some cosmic dust on the Witch's rocket . . .

This will stop her getting away.

The Witch decided it was time to leave.

Now you've left me stranded, you pest!

To make things worse, SuperTed took her magic ball.

Be nice to your new friends, Space Witch!

Just you wait, SuperTed!

Back at the treehouse . . .

Her magic ball will deal with our frogs, Spotty.

Eeeeek!

Make a. . .

HAPPY AND SAD

Bubbling blancmange! Here's Spotty to show you how to make a mask that's **double-dramatic!**

You will need:

- coloured card or stiff paper
- a paper plate
- two mini-yoghurt pots
- sticky tape and glue
- scissors
- felt tip pen
- elastic

1

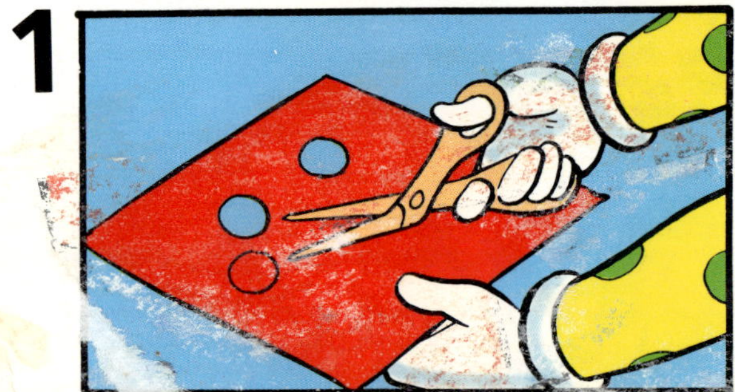

Take a piece of coloured card about 18cm square. Carefully cut out 2 eye-holes.

2

Cut the bottom off [illegible] of spotty pots and [illegible]

3

Stick the paper plate to the top of the mask as shown. Cut a slit as marked by the dotted lines.

4

Cross the two sides over slightly and secure them with a piece of sticky tape.

ROBOT MASK!

5

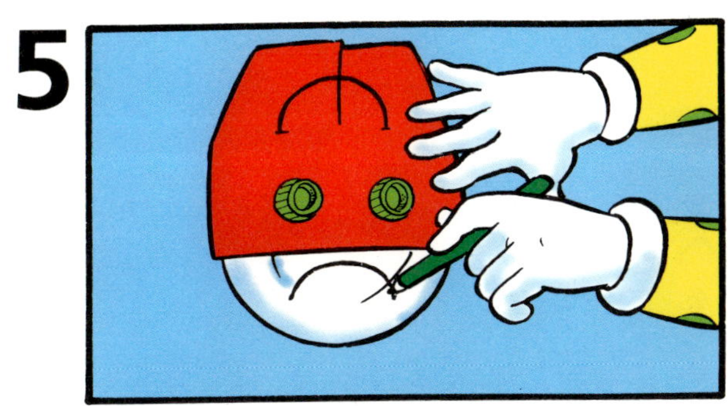

Draw a happy smile on the coloured card. Turn your mask round, and draw a sad mouth.

6

Use the rest of your coloured card to decorate your mask with ears and a long tongue!

7 Fix elastic to the sides and choose which way round to wear your mask!

Nippy Slippers

Nipper slippers are all the rage with the children . . . but are they quite what they seem . . .

Cre-ak! The door opened slowly and, from around the bottom corner, peered a weird little face. With big teeth, three eyes and a pointed ear that stuck out from a mop of frizzy, green hair on the top of its head, the creature began to slide silently into view.

"Great Moons of Spot!" gasped Spotty, leaping up from his chair. "W. . .What is it?"

Suddenly, there was the sound of giggling and a freckle-faced boy walked into the room. "It's a **slipper!** See? I'm wearing the other one, too!" laughed Tom. He held his other foot forward and showed Spotty how that slipper, too, was shaped like a crazy creature.

"Don't look so surprised, Spotty!" chuckled SuperTed. "It won't bite!"

"These furry Nipper Slippers are really **great!"** explained Tom. "Mum and Dad bought me a pair for Christmas! All the kids at school have them!"

Tom took one off to le[illegible] have a closer look. Spo[illegible] tested the slipper's sharp-looking teeth and saw they were only made of rubber.

"H'm! I don't suppose you can get a **spotty** pair, can you?" he asked.

"We'll see," replied SuperTed. "Right now, we ought to be going!"

"Thanks for visiting me, SuperTed!" said Tom.

"Yes, it's very kind of you!" his Mum smiled. "Tom's almost better now, but he has been very ill."

"Having his **hero** pay a surprise call has cheered him up no end!" added Tom's Dad.

"And so have those Nipper Slippers!" said SuperTed. "But I'm always pleased to help!"

As SuperTed and Spotty took off into the night sky, Spotty could hardly stop talking about the novelty slippers.

"I'll show you where they are made!" said SuperTed, zooming off towards the other side of town. But, even at that moment, the Nipper Slipper Factory had other unexpected visitors.

Meanwhile, Skeleton checked the night security officer was safely gagged and bound. Before long, Bulk had filled the sack and the three villains raced for their getaway van, outside. They had already forced open the factory gates and turned off the alarm system.

While Skeleton took the wheel, Tex snatched the sack from Bulk and peered inside. There were Nipper Slippers of every shape and size. But, suddenly, Tex's face turned almost as fierce and red as the freaky-faced slipper he held. "Bulk, you idiot! There's not a **pair** among them!"

"Be sure to get the **right** ones!" Tex barked, as Bulk headed for the store room, carrying a big, empty sack.

"Er, but, boss. . .!" began Bulk, looking puzzled.

"Don't argue, you dummy! These Nipper Slippers will earn us a fortune – especially when I **treble** the price of every pair!" chuckled Tex.

"But, boss," began Bulk, nervously, "you **told** me just to take the **right** ones. All the **left** slippers are still in the store room!"

Tex furiously swiped at Bulk with the slipper. "Gah! We'll have to go back and get them!" he snapped. But the cowboy crook's luck was even worse than he imagined. For hardly had he entered the factory again, when SuperTed and Spotty arrived, overhead.

"That's strange!" said SuperTed. "The factory gates should be locked up, at night! Come on. We'd better check!"

And when they did – very carefully and quietly – they soon found the night security officer, struggling to free himself. "It's Texas Pete and his gang!" he whispered to SuperTed, who removed the man's gag. "They're still here!"

"Then we'll make sure they don't **slipper** way!" said SuperTed.

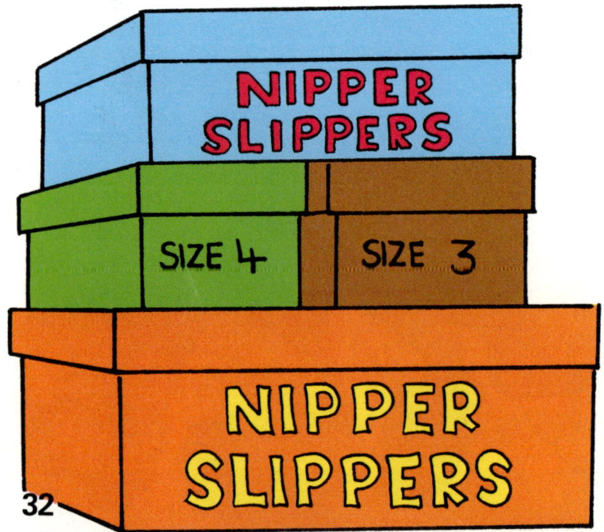

Moments later, he peered through a ventilator grill into the store room, where Tex and his cronies were emptying the shelves.

"Ready for action, Spotty?" whispered SuperTed. But Spotty pulled out a small bottle from his pocket. He removed the stopper and sprinkled some of its strange, popping, crackling contents through the grill.

"You said it, SuperTed. Luckily, I've got my **cosmic dust** with me. This should **liven** things up a bit!"

Sure enough, the cloud of magical dust settled on the Nipper Slippers – which instantly came to life! They flew out of the sack, whizzing and whirling around the room. All the while they 'snap, snapped, SNAPPED!' and made strange growling noises.

"R. . . run for it!" shouted Tex who, for a moment, caught one of the creature-like slippers in his cowboy hat. But the sharp-toothed slipper bit straight through it! "Before they have our hides!"

"D. . . did you say hide, boss?" gasped Bulk, diving into a big, empty storage bin and closing the lid. He was just in time – before a flying flock of the freaky slippers began to bash on the top of it. Another one kept swiping at Skeleton, making his bones rattle. Meanwhile, more Nipper Slippers nipped at Tex's trousers while he raced around the room, until he bumped straight into Skeleton.

"I think they've had enough!" chuckled SuperTed, spotting a large vacuum cleaner nearby. He plugged it in, and turned a switch to *'blow'*. Then he held the cleaner's tube-like head against the grill. A powerful jet of air blasted into the store room, blowing all the cosmic dust off the slippers – which instantly fell, lifeless, to the floor.

"Gah! SuperTed!" snarled Tex, as the very special bear entered the store room. Tex, Bulk and Skeleton were too exhausted to try and run.

"You can put all those slippers back on the shelves!" said SuperTed.

"But, first, they've some vacuuming to do!" added Spotty, bringing in the big cleaner. "They can collect up all my cosmic dust again, so I can put it back in my bottle!"

"Whatever you s. . .say!" shivered Skeleton. "As long as those Nipper Slippers don't move on their own again!"

"Agreed!" chuckled SuperTed. "They were very **nippy!** In fact, you could hardly see them for **dust!"**

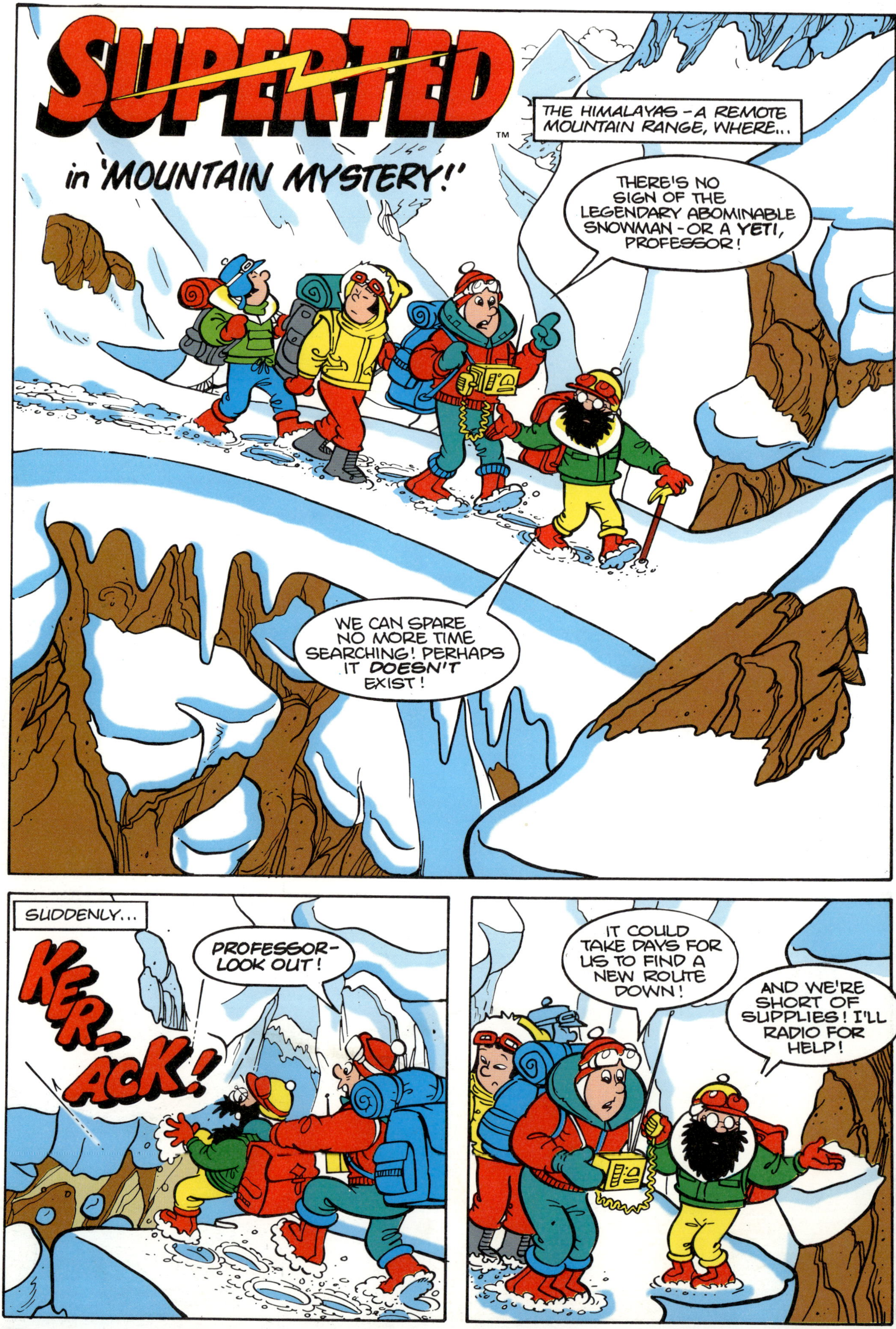

SUPERTED™

in 'MOUNTAIN MYSTERY!'

THE HIMALAYAS – A REMOTE MOUNTAIN RANGE, WHERE...

THERE'S NO SIGN OF THE LEGENDARY ABOMINABLE SNOWMAN – OR A **YETI**, PROFESSOR!

WE CAN SPARE NO MORE TIME SEARCHING! PERHAPS IT **DOESN'T** EXIST!

MEANWHILE, BY THEIR SECRET TREE-TOP HOUSE...
IF THAT'S MEANT TO LOOK LIKE ME, IT LEAVES ME COLD!
I THOUGHT IT WAS PRETTY ...ER...COOL!!

CAREFUL, SPOTTY! THAT SNOWFALL!
WHUMP!
OOPH!

SH-SH-SHIVERING SNOWBALLS!
HOLD IT, SPOTTY! THERE'S A MESSAGE COMING THROUGH!
CALLING SUPERTED... EMERGENCY...!

SHORTLY...
LET'S ROCKET TO RESCUE THE PROFESSOR, SPOTTY!
THAT SMOKE -IT'S A SIGNAL FLARE! THERE'S THE EXPEDITION!

WE'LL SOON GET YOU ACROSS, PROFESSOR! IT'S JUST A MATTER OF HOW TO...

...BRIDGE THAT GAP!
I'LL FIX ONE END TO THE SPOTTY ROCKET, SUPERTED!

WITH THE ROPE BRIDGE SECURE...
THAT'S EVERYONE SAFE, PROFESSOR. IT'S IT'S JUST KNOWING THE ROPES!
WE'VE BROUGHT YOU EXTRA FOOD, TOO!

THANKYOU, SUPERTED! WE'LL SOON REACH OUR BASE-CAMP NOW!
LOOKS LIKE THE FAMOUS YETI WILL REMAIN A MYSTERY, SPOTTY!
HMMM...

HUGE FOOTPRINTS! I WONDER WHERE THEY LEAD...? OOPS!
SLIP!

IT'S A CAVE AND...GREAT MOONS OF SPOT! I'VE R...REALLY SLIPPED UP!

NEXT MOMENT...
SO THAT'S WHERE YOU GOT SPOTTY! I...BUBBLING BLANCMANGE!
SUPERTED, WE'VE GOT COMPANY!

LUCKILY, SUPERTED CAN TALK TO ALL CREATURES...
HE'S THE YETI ALL RIGHT, SPOTTY! HIS NAME'S 'JETTY'! BUT HE'S VERY SHY - AND LONELY!
PERHAPS HE WANTS TO PLAY!

YOODEE-YOO!
THIS PUMP-UP SPACE-DINGHY FROM THE SPOTTY ROCKET MAKES A GREAT TOBOGGAN!
HE'S ENJOYING THIS! SO AM I!

CAREFUL, SPOTTY! OR WE'LL HIT THAT SNOWMAN!
JETTY YETI MUST LIKE BUILDING THEM AS MUCH AS I DO!

BUT...
WOOEEE -DOOBY!
PULSATING PLANETS! THAT'S NO SNOWMAN!
IT'S M... MOVING!

WE'RE GOING TO COLLIDE!
NOT IF I CAN HELP IT! HANG ON!
UGGA!

PHEW! THAT WAS LUCKY!
EVEN **LUCKIER** FOR JETTY - LOOKS AS IF HE'S FOUND A FRIEND!
COO-WOO-EE!

A PITY WE HAVE TO GO, SUPERTED! THE YETI SURE KNOW HOW TO BUILD SNOWMEN!
YES, AND THEY'RE DEFINITELY **NOT ABOMINABLE!**

TO THINK, WE DISCOVERED **TWO** YETI!
RIGHT, SPOTTY! ONLY WE WON'T TELL ANYONE - AT LEAST, NOT **YETI**! CHUCKLE!
THE END

Giants are only found in story books . . . aren't they?

Megamoon!

"Great moons of Spot!" gasped Spotty, as Superted finished telling him all about Jack and the Beanstalk. "I'd . . . hate to be chased by a giant, like poor Jack!"

"Don't worry, Spotty!" grinned SuperTed. "It's only a story. Besides, Jack **did** escape!" SuperTed closed the book he had been holding and, next moment, hurried off towards the space station's launch-chamber.

"Last one to the space scooter's a giant jelly!" he cried. "Come on! We've not had a single call for help from Earth all week. So let's go exploring!"

"Good idea!" replied Spotty, hurrying after SuperTed. "Only, please don't use that word **giant** again!"

VROOOSH! With SuperTed at the scooter's controls and Spotty clinging on tightly behind, the two friends took off into the star-spangled darkness. They soon left the space station far behind. Suddenly, SuperTed saw a meteorite storm speeding towards them.

"Hold tight, Spotty!" he called. "We're going to outride that hurtling heap of space rock!" SuperTed angled the space scooter away. He made it dip and weave, twist, turn and roll – until Spotty felt his tummy doing the same!

"Whoopee!" yelled SuperTed, as they finally flew clear. "That beats a roller-coaster ride, any day!"

"Maybe!" replied Spotty. "But d. . .do you mind if we land somewhere until everything's stopped spinning – including my head!"

"How about that moon, over there?" said SuperTed, pointing and, very soon, they landed on its bright yellow surface.

"I've never been here before," said Spotty, slowly and shakily stepping off the scooter. "At least it looks quiet. I'll rest under that green tree-trunk."

But as Spotty leant against it, SuperTed stared in amazement. "Blistering bananas!" he gasped. "That's no tree. It's the stem of a **giant** flower!"

"Did you say **g...giant?"** muttered Spotty, uneasily.

"And that's not all!" added SuperTed. "Look! There's a mega-sized mushroom!"

Spotty swallowed hard as they saw that everything growing around them was enormous. He recalled the story of Jack and the Beanstalk. "Then if anyone lives here, they'd be huge, too! I thought you s...said you only found giants in s...stories!"

Hardly had he spoken, when they heard a strange sniffing and snorting. "Watch out, Spotty!" called SuperTed, as two big purple eyes and a long snout appeared between some massive leaves. The creature's round, prickly body was even bigger – andthe end of each prickle glowed like a lightbulb.

"I think it's a sort of hedgehog!" began SuperTed.

"I'm a **hedgehog** – anyone knows that!" replied the creature. "And there's no need to stare! There are lots of us on Megamoon!"

"Sorry!" said SuperTed. "We're visitors and. . .!"

A thud, **thud, THUD** interrupted him. It was very loud and made the ground shake. The hedgehog hurried off.

"It s...sounds like giant footsteps!" said Spotty, nervously.

"Time we...er...stepped on it!" replied SuperTed. "Back to the space scooter – and fast."

As they raced towards it, the footsteps grew louder and louder. Spotty did not dare to look. They climbed aboard and took off. But, suddenly, a towering figure loomed over them.

"Bubbling blancmange!" yelled SuperTed, trying to turn the scooter in mid-air. Too late! A huge hand scooped them up!

"Coming here was a mega mistake!" said SuperTed, struggling to free himself.

"I wish we had a beanstalk to escape down!" said Spotty, glimpsing at the ground far below.

SuperTed forced his head between the giant's fingers and called up to him. "I'm SuperTed. You must let us go!"

"DON'T BE AFRAID!" a voice boomed like a drum. "I have heard of you, SuperTed. It's lucky I saw you. I need your help!"

"You d...do?" gasped Spotty. "I mean, you don't want to **eat** us?"

The giant laughed until his whole body shook. SuperTed and Spotty had to cover their ears. Now they saw he had red cheeks, a long, glowing nose, and seemed perfectly friendly.

"Of course not! I only wish I were as **small** as you two!" said the giant, who told them his name was Glownor. "Then I could rescue the sparkle-stone which fell from my wife's wedding ring. It dropped into a tiny crack in the ground. It's too deep for me to reach with my big fingers and the ground is so hard, I can't dig it up!"

"Leave it to us, Glownor!" said SuperTed. And, very soon, he had squeezed into the narrow gap and was rocketing down and down. Using his back pack, Spotty flew close behind. Meanwhile, Glownor knelt over the small hole, so his glowing nose lit the way.

"There's the sparkle-stone!" called SuperTed, at last, as it sparkled below them. With Spotty's help, and using all his special strength, the Superbear carried it back to Glownor.

The giant's wife was very pleased. "You must stay for tea!" she said.

"Well, I am feeling peckish!" said Spotty.

But he and SuperTed had quite forgotten how much giants eat. There was a mountain of sandwiches, enough fizzy drink to fill a swimming pool and a colourful cake the size of SuperTed's space station.

"That's what I call an enormous meal!" laughed Spotty.

"A really **giant**-sized treat!" chuckled SuperTed. "See, Spotty! Not all giants mean **big** trouble!"

The End

SuperTed's favourite colour is orange, and his favourite **orange** is a. . .

JELLY ORANGE!

How to make one:

- Ask a grown up to help you make up some orange jelly.
- Help by stirring the jelly cubes round and round to make them melt.

- The jelly should be poured into half an orange skin.
- When the jelly has set hard, cut the orange skins in half – and eat the jelly! Delicious!

SLUURP!

MMMM!

Spotty's Special Pet

Spotty put the little creature carefully into his pocket and flew back to the treehouse to show SuperTed . . .
What are you going to do with it, Spotty?
I'm going to make him my pet.

Then Spotty looked for somewhere to keep him . . .
There! You'll be nice and cosy in this old cosmic dust bottle!
But then . . .
Great Moons of Spot!
There must have been some dust left in that bottle!

No sooner was the spotty creature free than he returned to his normal size.
I still think you should take him back, Spotty!
But Spotty was sure he could make his new pet learn to love him. Only . . .
Now he's taken my apple!

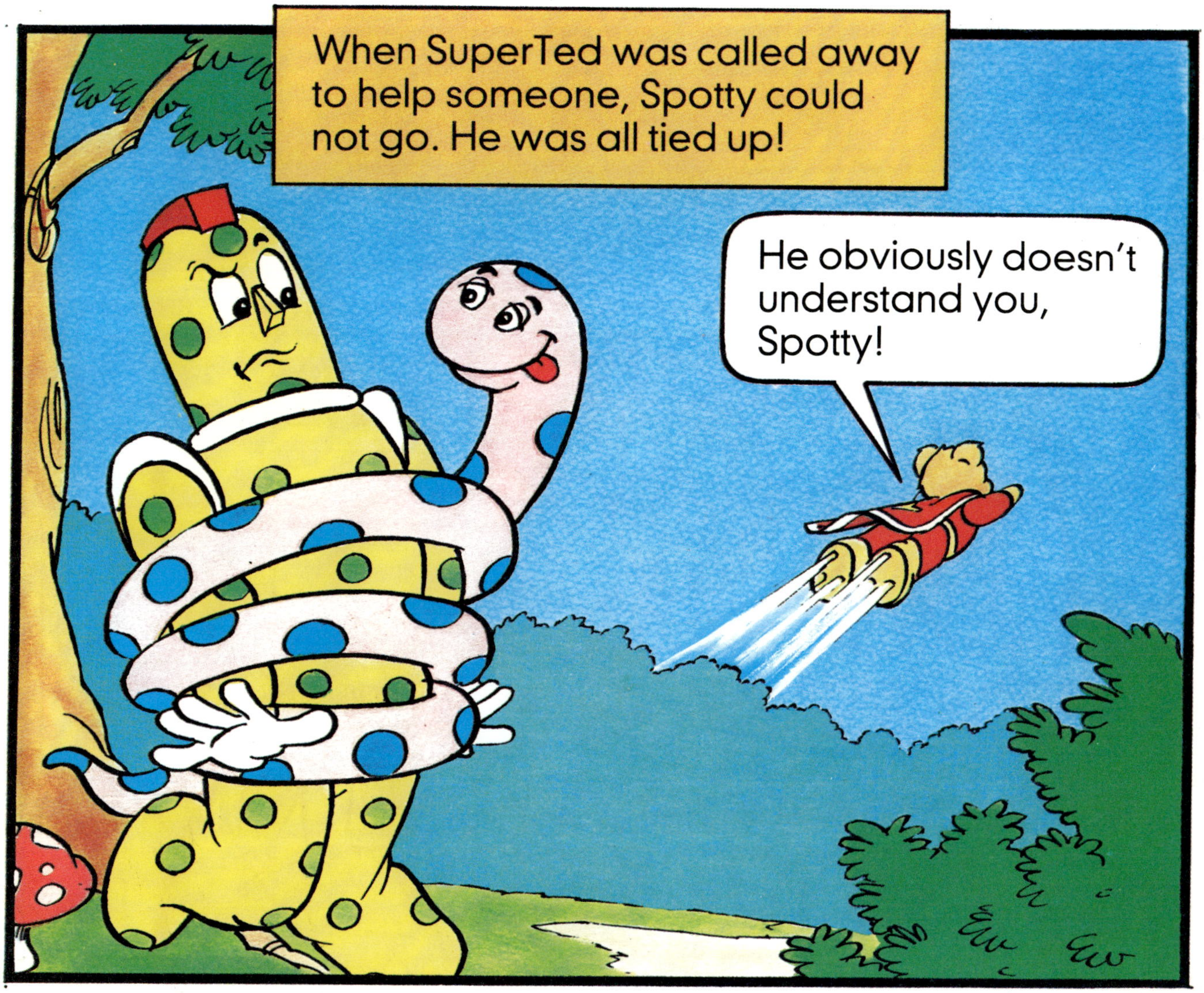

When SuperTed was called away to help someone, Spotty could not go. He was all tied up!

He obviously doesn't understand you, Spotty!

Very gently Spotty put a collar round his little pet . . .
There. Now we can go for a nice walk in the forest.
Only the creature decided to fly.
There's a good spotty creature.

But in the next second . . .
. . . he shrank!
Oh, dear! Where's he gone now?

Spotty heard a gurgle and turned . . .
Come back here at once! You're being very naughty!
Although he was only small, Spotty's pet could move very quickly . . .
He must get tired soon!

Before Spotty could catch him, the little creature floated up towards the treehouse . . .
Oh no! SuperTed's rolled up the ladder. How can I get back in the treehouse?
But Spotty's pet had other surprises to come. For once, he seemed to understand . . .
Now what are you up to?

Just then, SuperTed came home again . . .
He's helping me into the treehouse!
All right, little one. Even though I love you, I'm taking you, back to where I found you!

Spotty's Spot!
Whooshing along on a mega-space ride.
Look out! Poor Spotty's trying to hide!
Quick! Join the dots, he's rigid with fright!
Then make sure they're not left in black and white!

SuperTed and Spotty remember a very special, Christmas adventure!

The Christmas Presents!

"**Speeding sputnicks!**" gasped Spotty, as he searched through a pile of presents by the Christmas tree in their secret tree-top house. "It **must** be here somewhere!"

"Don't worry!" grinned SuperTed, looking up from sticking a label marked **TO TEXAS PETE!** on a big, brightly-wrapped gift. "There is a present for you, too!"

"It's my bottle of cosmic dust I'm looking for!" replied Spotty. "I can't find it anywhere!"

"Don't tell me you've wrapped it up with the presents – like you did last year?" chuckled SuperTed. "Remember? But it certainly came in handy when we had to help a very important person, indeed! Do you remember?"

For a moment, Spotty and SuperTed sat watching the sparkling Christmas tree lights as they recalled that extra-special adventure. . .

"Ho, Prancer! Run, Rudolph! Go, my beauties!" Santa Claus called to his reindeer, as they raced happily onwards, pulling his sleigh across the night sky. Stars twinkled, as if winking, and a silvery moon lit the way. Below, was the frozen world of the North Pole and Santa could feel the cold air on his red cheeks. But his thick red coat, hat and gloves kept him warm – and so did his big, white beard. His present-packed sleigh was hung with bells which sang a magical tune.

Suddenly, though, there was a crackling flash of white light. It sped past the reindeer, startling them. As they reared up in alarm, the sleigh jolted.

"Steady, Comet! Be calm, Donner!" called Santa, struggling with the reins. "It's only a shooting star!"

Too late! Santa's huge sack rolled, breaking open, and lots of presents cascaded out. Below, was a deep, dark crevasse in the ice and the presents fell down, down . . . into it.

"There's only one person who can help me get them," thought Santa, as he turned the sleigh back towards his Grotto.

"Santa calling SuperTed!" came the urgent message, as Santa's worried face appeared on the TV screen in the tree-top house. SuperTed could hardly believe it! Neither could Spotty, who looked up from where he had just found his bottle of cosmic dust, mistakenly wrapped up with their Christmas presents.

In no time, they were speeding northwards, leaving the lights of a million homes far behind.

"We haven't much time, if Santa's to deliver all those presents by Christmas Day!" said Spotty.

"We've only one chance!" replied SuperTed. "Spotty, just keep a tight hold on that cosmic dust of yours – and don't lose it again!"

As they landed on the snow, beside the crevasse, Santa Claus was waiting. So were his reindeer. Spotty had never seen any before and stared at their beautiful antlers.

"That crevasse is very deep. Somehow, we've got to reach all those presents down there!" said Santa, pointing into the yawing gap in the ice.

"Maybe we can get **them** to come to **us**!" said SuperTed. "Spotty, hand me that bottle of cosmic dust!"

Next moment, SuperTed pulled out the stopper and sprinkled some of the magical dust down into the crevasse.

"How will that help?" asked Santa, puzzled. "I don't see. . .!"

Just then, what he did see made Santa laugh with delight. The presents came flying up out of the crevasse, coated in the glittering, popping dust which brought them to life! They flew this way and that, while Santa's reindeer looked startled again.

"Now let's go catch those presents and . . . er . . . **wrap up** this whole affair, Spotty!" called SuperTed.

"Wait! Use these! It will be easier!" called Santa. He took out three large nets, with long handles, from among the gifts that remained on his sleigh.

"It's better than catching crooks!" laughed Spotty, as he scooped two presents into his net in one go. Santa joined in, too. His reindeer sped through the air, chasing the flying presents which he quickly caught. SuperTed was just as busy. So, before long, all the presents were safely in nets. SuperTed and Spotty zoomed alongside Santa's airborne sleigh and fixed the nets, like strange Christmas flags, behind it.

"Keep going, Santa!" called SuperTed. "As you fly along, the breeze will blow the cosmic dust off the presents – and they'll be back to normal again!"

"Thank you, SuperTed! Thank you, Spotty!" replied Santa, waving goodbye. "Happy Christmas!"

"It certainly was an unusual one!" recalled SuperTed, tying a big, bright ribbon around the parcel he had labelled for Texas Pete. Just then, Spotty jumped up and hurried across the room to the mantelpiece where a large, spotted sock was hanging. He reached inside it and took out the bottle of cosmic dust which he had lost.

"I just remembered! I put it in that sock I'd hung up for Santa!" he laughed. "Well, at least it's safe **this** Christmas – for the **present!"** replied SuperTed.

Then Spotty pointed to the parcel SuperTed had prepared for Tex. "Talking of presents, what is in that one?"

"What else, but a game for Tex, called: **MAKE A MILLION**! After all," SuperTed explained, "if he can play at being rich, it might make him stop stealing other folk's money! Ha-Ha-Ha!"

JOIN THE DOTS!